AXOLOTLS

Emma Bassier

DiscoverRoo
An Imprint of Pop!
popbooksonline.com

abdobooks.com

Published by Pop!, a division of ABDO, PO Box 398166, Minneapolis, Minnesota 55439. Copyright © 2020 by POP, LLC. International copyrights reserved in all countries. No part of this book may be reproduced in any form without written permission from the publisher. Pop!™ is a trademark and logo of POP, LLC.

Printed in the United States of America, North Mankato, Minnesota.

102019
012020

THIS BOOK CONTAINS RECYCLED MATERIALS

Cover Photo: Shutterstock Images
Interior Photos: Shutterstock Images, 1, 5, 6, 8, 11, 12, 13, 14, 17 (top), 17 (bottom), 19, 20–21, 22, 23, 25, 27, 28, 29, 30, 31; iStockphoto, 7, 15, 16–17; Red Line Editorial, 9; Pete Oxford/Minden Pictures/Newscom, 16 (top), 16 (bottom); Tomas Bravo/Reuters/Newscom, 26

Editor: Nick Rebman
Series Designer: Jake Slavik

Library of Congress Control Number: 2019942615
Publisher's Cataloging-in-Publication Data

Names: Bassier, Emma, author.

Title: Axolotls / by Emma Bassier

Description: Minneapolis, Minnesota : Pop!, 2020 | Series: Weird and wonderful animals | Includes online resources and index.

Identifiers: ISBN 9781532166020 (lib. bdg.) | ISBN 9781644943328 (pbk.) | ISBN 9781532167348 (ebook)

Subjects: LCSH: Axolotls--Juvenile literature. | Amphibians--Juvenile literature. | Oddities--Juvenile literature. | Amphibians--Behavior--Juvenile literature. | Salamanders--Juvenile literature.

Classification: DDC 597.85--dc23

WELCOME TO
DiscoverRoo!

Pop open this book and you'll find QR codes loaded with information, so you can learn even more!

Scan this code* and others like it while you read, or visit the website below to make this book pop!

popbooksonline.com/axolotls

*Scanning QR codes requires a web-enabled smart device with a QR code reader app and a camera.

TABLE OF
CONTENTS

CHAPTER 1
AN AMAZING AMPHIBIAN

An axolotl grabs a caterpillar in its mouth. The caterpillar struggles as the axolotl slowly swallows it. After eating, the axolotl rests. Its body blends in with

WATCH A VIDEO HERE!

An axolotl eats a caterpillar.

the murky water. Its greenish-brown skin

has gray spots.

Axolotls are also known as Mexican walking fish and water monsters.

Axolotls are **amphibians**. Most amphibians live in water when they are young. Then their bodies change,

and they start living on land. However, axolotls are different from most amphibians. They live their whole lives in water.

This canal in Mexico City was once home to many axolotls. Very few remain today.

In the wild, axolotls are found only in the **canals** of Mexico City. They live in fresh water. Unlike ocean water, fresh water does not have any salt in it.

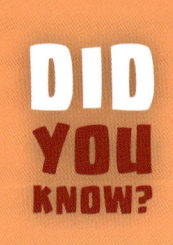

DID YOU KNOW?

Axolotls are named after Xolotl, the Aztec god of lightning. He could turn into an axolotl to escape from his enemies.

RANGE MAP

UNITED STATES

MEXICO

GULF OF
MEXICO

Mexico City

Axolotl range

GUATEMALA

PACIFIC
OCEAN

N
W E
S

CHAPTER 2
SOFT BODIES

Axolotls are a type of salamander. Most axolotls are 6 inches (15 cm) long. But some grow to be 12 inches (30 cm) long. Axolotls typically weigh 2 to 8 ounces (57–227 g). Females are usually larger than males.

LEARN MORE HERE!

Most axolotls are the size of an adult human's hand.

An axolotl's gills look like fuzzy hairs.

An axolotl's head is large and flat.

Feathery **gills** stick out from the back

and sides of the head. An adult axolotl

has four legs with webbed feet. Its tail is

long. The tail has a fin along the back.

Tiger salamanders get their name from their stripes, which are similar to a tiger's.

Adult axolotls look very similar to young axolotls.

Unlike most **amphibians**,

an axolotl does not go through a

metamorphosis. As a result, it does

not lose any body parts when it becomes an adult. Instead, it keeps its gills and tail for its whole life. However, it does grow lungs and legs.

A tadpole looks very different from an adult frog.

WHAT IS METAMORPHOSIS?

Metamorphosis is a change that happens to some animals during growth. Most amphibians, such as frogs, go through a metamorphosis. Their bodies lose some parts when they change from tadpoles to adults. Tadpoles swim through water with their tails. They breathe with gills. But adult frogs hop with legs. They breathe with lungs.

LIFE CYCLE OF AN AXOLOTL

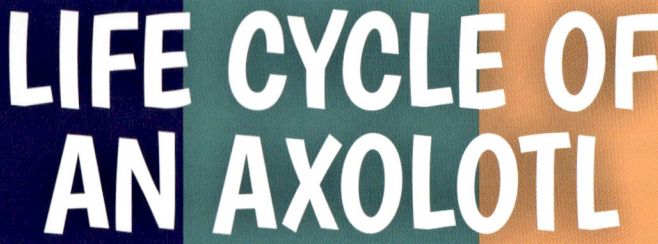

The eggs hatch into tadpoles. Each tadpole has gills and a tail.

Adult female axolotls lay eggs.

As the tadpole grows larger, it becomes an adult. It grows lungs and legs, but it does not lose its gills or tail.

Axolotls live up to 15 years in the wild.

CHAPTER 3
FORMING NEW LIMBS

An axolotl uses its legs to crawl along **canal** bottoms. To swim, it wiggles its body. It waves its tail back and forth. Its front legs paddle and steer.

COMPLETE AN ACTIVITY HERE!

An axolotl can swim at speeds of approximately 1 mile per hour (1.6 km/h).

DID YOU KNOW? Axolotls appear to be dancing when they mate.

Axolotls mostly breathe with their **gills**. However, they can also breathe with their lungs. Like other **amphibians**, axolotls use their

An axolotl cools off in the shade.

surroundings to help control their body
temperature. Sunlight helps them stay
warm. Shade under rocks helps them
stay cool.

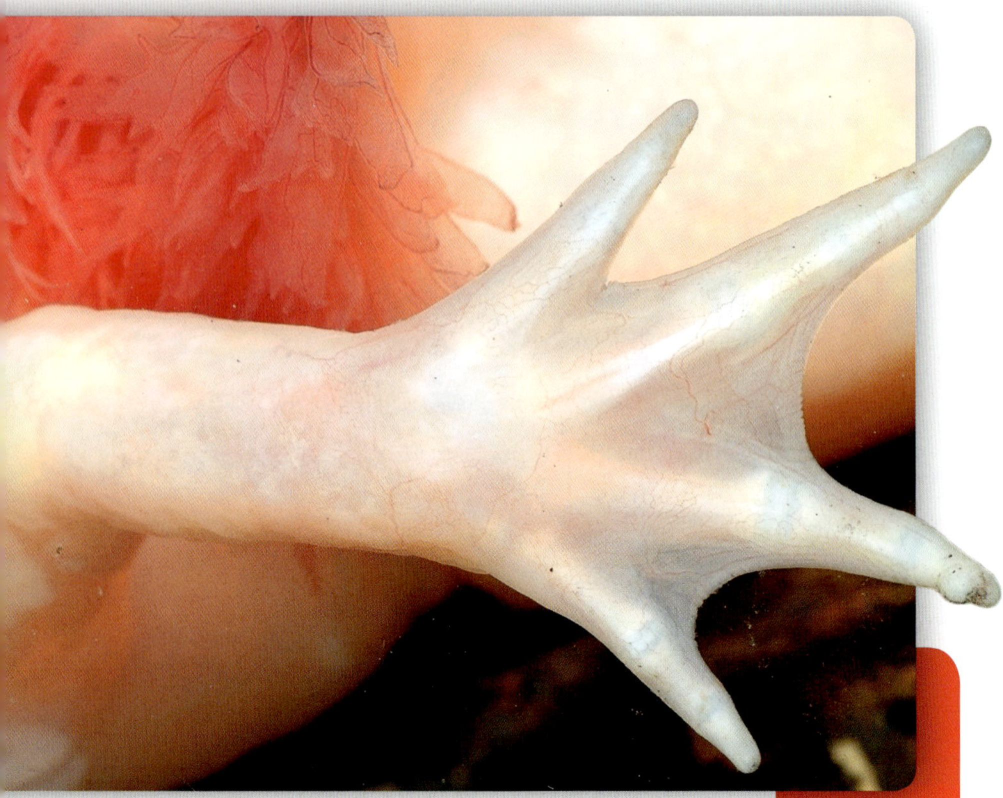

An axolotl will not die if it loses a leg.

Axolotls can **regenerate** many body parts. They can regrow missing legs, tails, and some organs. They can even regrow parts of their brains.

Regeneration helps axolotls survive.

They can keep living after being injured.

DID YOU KNOW?

An axolotl can regrow an entire limb in 40 days.

Two axolotls make their way through the water.

CHAPTER 4
AXOLOTLS IN DANGER

Axolotls eat worms, tiny insects, small fish, and crustaceans. Crustaceans are shelled animals that live in the water.

Axolotls spend most of their time along the bottoms of **canals**. Living in

LEARN MORE HERE!

An axolotl eats a meal of young insects.

deep, dark waters protects them from

being eaten by large birds.

Scientists search for axolotls in the canals of Mexico City.

Polluted water is a threat to

axolotls. Large storms push waste into

Mexico City's canals. The unclean water

can kill axolotls. They breathe it in

through their skin or **gills**.

Pollution is a major problem in Mexico City's canals.

Tilapia have caused the number of axolotls to decrease sharply.

Carp and tilapia are other threats. These fish eat axolotls. Carp and tilapia are not **native** to Mexico City's waters. Humans brought them there in the 1980s.

Today, people are trying to save axolotls. For example, people have set aside areas where carp and tilapia cannot live. That way, the fish cannot eat the axolotls.

MAKING CONNECTIONS

TEXT-TO-SELF

Axolotls live in Mexico City. What animals have you seen in or near the place you live?

TEXT-TO-TEXT

Have you read other books about animals that live in water? How are those animals similar to or different from axolotls?

TEXT-TO-WORLD

Axolotls are endangered because of polluted water and non-native fish. How can people help endangered animals?

GLOSSARY

amphibian – an animal that lives fully underwater when it is young and then grows to be able to live on land.

canal – a waterway made by humans.

gill – a part on an animal's body that helps it breathe underwater.

metamorphosis – a complete change in an animal's body.

native – naturally living in a certain area.

polluted – unclean because of harmful chemicals or garbage.

regenerate – to regrow.

INDEX

ONLINE RESOURCES
popbooksonline.com

Scan this code* and others like it while you read, or visit the website below to make this book pop!

popbooksonline.com/axolotls

*Scanning QR codes requires a web-enabled smart device with a QR code reader app and a camera.